Grandmothers Are Very Special People

Compiled by
Mary Carey

THE C. R. GIBSON COMPANY
Norwalk, Connecticut

The Happy Affair

The happiest love affair—the one which will never grow stale or tiresome or end in bitterness—is the one between a grandmother and her grandchild. It is usually love at first sight, and the infatuation only deepens on each side as the child grows. It can last for a lifetime; men and women often remember best the warm joy of having had a grandmother, or perhaps a great-grandmother.

Mary Carey

"What A Grandmother Is "

The great authorities on grand-mothers are children. Any child can give a perfect explanation of what a grandmother is. No two explanations will be alike, but then no two grandmothers are exactly alike.

In 1967, a young lady named Patsy Gray (she was nine years old) wrote this masterly composition.

A grandmother is a lady who has no children of her own, so she likes other people's little girls. A grand-father is a man grandmother. He goes for walks with boys, and they talk about fishing and tractors and like that.

Grandmas don't have to do anything except be there. They are old, so they shouldn't play hard or run. It is enough if they drive us to the market where the pretend horse is and have lots of dimes ready. Or if they take us for walks, they slow down past things like pretty leaves or caterpillars. They should never say "Hurry up."

Usually they are fat, but not too fat to tie the kids' shoes. They wear glasses, and they can take their teeth and gums off. It is better if they don't typewrite or play cards, except with us. They don't have to be smart, only answer questions like why dogs chase cats or how come God isn't married.

They don't talk baby talk like visitors do, because it is hard to understand. When they read to us they don't skip words or mind if it is the same story again.

Everybody should try to have one, especially if you don't have television, because grandmas are the only grownups who have time.

The
Granny Glass

When my grandma reads to me,
    She has a special glass,
And through that magic lens I see
    The tigers in the grass.

She holds me safe. I am not chilled
    By snow on distant mountains,
And through her special reading glass
    Come dancing colored fountains.

I cuddle close and we soar high
    Upon the backs of eagles.
We look down upon ancient lands
    With castles tall and regal.

Before one story ends, we see
    A pumpkin coach dash by.
Then Grandma reads about a vine
    That grows up to the sky.

When I'm alone I try to make
    Enchantments come to pass,
But magic seems to happen best
    When Grandma holds the glass.

Lee Sobelman

Very Special Gifts

Grandmothers are noted for giving gifts. Here Margaret Mead talks of two gifts received from her grandmother. One was her teachings; the other, time—a whole century.

The grandmother who lived with us was my father's mother. Looking back, I realize that she gave me an extra century of life through the tales she told me about the little town of Winchester, Ohio, where she had grown up. Although it was 60 years before I myself saw Winchester, Grandma made every person, every house, every nook and cranny and the whole style of living familiar to me.

She read me books she had read as a child and books my father had read. She told me, in a voice that I had learned I could fully trust, how times had changed. She explained to me about the telegraph, the first automobile and the men who were then just beginning to link far places in a new way, by flying.

All her life my grandmother had been a teacher, experimental, curious and exploratory, avid for new ideas on how to open the minds of small children. She taught me algebra before arithmetic and wherever we went for our summer holidays she had me make a herbarium, using new methods to preserve the colors and outlines of plants.

She talked and I listened, and I talked and she listened. Later she used to tell me that after I had chattered to her all day, when evening came and the day's work was done, I would say to her in an expectant voice, "Now let's sit down and talk."

It is hard to know which is more important for a grandparent to do—talk or listen. But adults must keep time—the years before the child was born—firmly in mind. When Edward VII died, my grandmother sighed, "Poor boy, he had so little time to be king." But she did not ask whether I remembered Queen Victoria. She knew exactly what I knew and what had to be explained to me. She kept the rhythm of my life in her head.

Whose Baby? A Brief Introduction To Grandparents

You are truly a kindly person, your misanthropy is
    mostly like a sleeping volcano, like Mauna Loa,
But one thing that awakens it is other people's chil-
    dren, than which you rate no flora or fauna
    lower,
So you have spent much of your life cultivating tact
    and forbearance
And the art of avoiding other people's children
    without offending their parents,
And just when your allergy to other people's chil-
    dren is recognized by those of your friends who
    seem out to emulate the old woman who lived
    in a shoe,
Why, along come your grandchildren, who are cer-
    tainly other people's children if you grant that
    your own children are people, which some
    broadminded parents do,
And as sure as the filbert is named after St. Phili-
    bert and is a cultivated variety of hazel,
Your attitude towards other people's children un-
    dergoes a swift reappraisal.
You ask yourself, trying to be detached and distant,
If instead of rejecting these little strangers you
    idolized them, are you being inconsistent?
No indeed, you sensibly conclude that these particu-
    lar little strangers are the exception to the rule,

Because even when they are mewling and regurgitating in their nurse's arms it's a beguiling regurgitation and a melodious mewl.

You are in a euphoric humor,

You are tempted to dismiss their parents as mere middlemen, necessary only to deliver the finished product to the ultimate consumer,

So you mistrust not only their parents, but their pediatrician, you become a chronic worrier,

And of their favor you become a shameless currier.

You want fire engines and ambulances kept off the street and the entire work of the household to cease during their slumbers.

And you engage in expensive undeclared competition for their affection with their other grandparents, your opposite numbers.

Eventually you try to adjust your conduct to the greatest handicap a grandparent endures,

The fact that they are other people's, not yours,

So you say to yourself, Hands off, and you promise yourself that the most heartless treatment of them will leave you silent as the grave,

And then you find yourself defending them against their parents next time they misbehave.

There is a proverb often quoted by young Married Couples in China, both Nationalist and Indo—:

When grandparents enter door, discipline fly out window.

Ogden Nash

Simply Love

The greatest gift that the old have to offer and receive from the young is love. The children get from their great-grandmother an unqualified, undemanding affection that does not say, "I love you because you are good or quiet or neat or clever." It simply says, "I love you because you are here." And the youngest do not feel, as they are sometimes encouraged to feel with their parents, "I love you because you take care of me or buy me things I want." Their response is more, "I love you because you love me." In a world where emotions are so often complicated by considerations of need and dependency, we ought not to deny our children and old people the simple pleasures of sharing undemanding affection.

Abby Avin Belson

I Like Your Face, Gram

Grandparents and grandchildren who are truly close, accepting one another with a love that is uncritical and undemanding, achieve an intimacy unlike any other. Ernest Buckler describes such a relationship in his book, "Ox Bells and Fireflies."

The child is six. The grandmother is eighty.

"Gram, what makes so many cracks in your face?"

"Cracks?"

"Yes. There's *more* . . . when you laugh like that."

"Yes, you can get them from laughing. I did laugh a lot. And you can get them from . . . I suppose I got some of them from the day the well your grandfather was rocking up caved in on him and I heard him scream just once for me to come help, but I couldn't see where he was . . . and from the day the forest fires were so thick around us the cinders were lighting on the roof, until some miracle sent the rain, and . . . "

"Do you get them from bein married?"

"Yes. But they're the best kind. The worst

kind's the kind you get when you've got nothing to trouble you. Not a husband. Not a chick nor a child. When there's no one you can say 'What would you do?' to, when you're puzzled."

"Will I get them some day?"

"Yes, child. You likely will. But don't you worry. You'll have things happen to you, I can see. You'll make things happen. You'll have the best kind of wrinkles in your face."

"I didn't mean I didn't like your face, Gram."

"I know, child."

"When we have something special for supper you slip some offa your plate onto mine, don't you."

"Sometimes."

"And when I want to do something they can't see why I want to do it, you know why, the very first one, don't you. And when it's too cold to say my prayers on the floor, you let me say them in bed, don't you. And when I tore the whole seat outa my pants slidin down the shop roof into the big drift, you just laughed, didn't you."

"Yes."

"I didn't mean I didn't like your face, Gram."

"I know, child, I know."

"You laughed, didn't you. We can always make each other laugh, can't we."

A New Grandmother's Prayer

Dear Lord, Who's excited about a first grandchild? Me.

Please, Lord, forgive my being ungrammatical— but, after four sons, to have a girl in the family . . .

Dear Lord, Thank you for sending my husband and me a girl, on the second time around.

Please make Pamela Jamie strong and healthy. Size 10 will do, thank you. And see that she plays bridge, tennis, and the piano—the zither, if she insists. And learns to cook and dance and has an inquisitive mind and is a good citizen.

And please, Lord, a sense of humor, too.

Dear Lord, Thank you for helping me cross that gap between Month Number Nine and Cloud Seven. And do you really think it's too early to book Lester Lanin's orchestra for her coming-out party?

Please help her, when she's a big girl, learn to wear the kind of clothes that will make people ask, "Who is she?" not "Who does she think she is?"

And please help her to stand up for her rights, without, at the same time, stamping on somebody else's foot.

Dear Lord, Please see that Pamela Jamie calls Grandma and Grandpa at least once a week, if only to say, "Goo-goo,"

and even if it's only to get her parents off her back. What if she does reverse the charges?

And please see that, in due time, she has a few diamonds and a bit of ermine—only because the color is so neutral, and neither ever hurts a woman's looks.

And, Lord, please see to it also that the beauty salons need Pamela Jamie more than she needs them.

Dear Lord, Please find nice girls for our three other sons, so Pamela Jamie can start having cousins.

And thanks for having had somebody give birth to a baby boy about four or five years ago, a boy who will grow up to be good enough for Pamela.

And please see that he studies and doesn't run around with other girls.

And please, Lord, don't convince us that the sun rises in the east and sets in the west— and not upon Pamela Jamie.

Dear Lord, See that she shows good legs.

And please don't let her find out for a while that although her thumb measures less than an inch, she has her grandparents firmly under it.

Please, Lord, see that she marries happily and young and that they invite us to the wedding.

And help us on the project for my Great-Grandmother's Prayer.

Dear Lord, Can't you make it less than nine months next time? I can't stand suspense movies even when I know who did it.

Please, Lord, help her have a bright and healthy and useful life, our Pamela Jamie.

And for this 'pink, six-and-a-half-pound favor, Dear Lord, we humbly thank Thee.

Sylvia R. Lyons

Advice On Visiting A New Grandmother

Prepare to exclaim over dozens of
    snapshots—
        Crib shots,
            Bib shots,
                Nap shots,
                    And lap shots.
Sing praises to dear little what-you-may-call-it
Whose charms are enshrined in his grandmother's
    wallet!

—Jean Conder Soule

Spoiling: Part Of The Fun

Of course grandmothers indulge their grandchildren. That's part of what it's all about. And any child who doesn't have a grand- mother should run right out and adopt one, so that he can be prop- erly petted and pampered. Even Dr. Benjamin Spock agrees.

Many grandparents are accused of spoiling their grandchildren, and of course this is true. But I don't think there is too much harm in this as long as the grandparents keep the children's respect. Perhaps it would be desirable for every one of us—old as well as young—to be spoiled by at least one person as a salve for all the bruises and demands of life. Just be- cause you are spoiled by one individual doesn't mean that you become a corrupted character; you know that you can't get away with spoiled behavior with the rest of your relatives and the world.

Afternoon With Grandmother

I always shout when Grandma comes,
But Mother says, "Now please be still
And good and do what *Grandma* wants."
And I say, "Yes, I will."

So off we go in Grandma's car.
"There's a brand new movie quite near by,"
She says, "that I'd rather like to see."
And I say, "So would I."

The show has horses and chases and battles;
We gasp and hold hands the whole way through.
She smiles and says, "I liked that lots."
And I say, "I did, too."

"It's made me hungry, though," she says,
"I'd like a malt and tarts with jam.
By any chance are you hungry, too?"
And I say, "Yes, I am."

Later at home my Mother says,
"I hope you were careful to do as bid.
Did you and Grandma have a good time?"
And I say, "YES, WE DID!!!"

Barbara Huff

Grandmothers Get All
The Breaks

My mother is looking awfully chipper lately. Her eyes are bright; her complexion is rosy; her smile is dazzling and there's a spring in her step.

I, on the other hand, am looking wintry. After a day of refereeing the older children (in between my own bouts with a baby who won't stand still), I feel and look like last week's half-melted snowman.

"Are you Grandma's mommy?" my five-year-old asked me not so long ago.

"No," I told her. "I just feel that way."

The exchange set me thinking. Of all the double-barreled words in the English language, none is more to the point than that one. A grandmother is a mother who is having a grand time because her children are grown up. My eldest child being seven, I have an excellent chance of getting there in fifteen years. I can hardly wait.

By that time, my handbag will no longer be stuffed with PTA notices, broken shoe laces, spare mittens, popped buttons, pediatrician's prescriptions, teething biscuits and coupons to be mailed with fifteen cents for a free cardboard racing car, unassembled. I will carry only snapshots of my grandchildren. I'll take the praise, their parents can tote the paraphernalia.

My car will be free of car seats, car beds, diaper-changing kits, ballet costumes, ice skates, rock collections and children to be picked up and delivered on a day-long schedule. I will have plenty of room and plenty of time to take my grandchildren driving—when I'm in the mood.

My house will be empty—spacious without its current clutter of cereal boxes to be cut into farmyard animals, sneakers to be grown into and out of, socks to be darned, school dresses to be taken up or let down, toys to be repaired, little friends to be sent home after lunch and other little friends to be kept till after dinner. I'll be delighted to have my grandchildren visit—a few at a time—and even more delighted, probably, when their parents come to take them home.

When my mother became a grandmother, she was a middle-aged lady. I remember the day she came breathlessly into my hospital room, tears of joy in her eyes. "My baby!" she cried. Only it wasn't me she was looking at.

She took up residence outside the nursery window and has been, ever since, my children's best friend and most outspoken admirer. By the time my third baby arrived, my mother was no longer middle-aged; she had grown young—so young in fact that people kept thinking she was the baby's mother. "Your baby's hair is the same color as yours," another visitor remarked one day as mother stood beaming into the hospital nursery.

"Thank you, but it's my daughter's baby," Mother replied, "and *my* hair color comes out of a bottle."

Ah yes, while mothers get gray, grandmothers get gay. It is this gaiety—plus lavishings of love and lollipops—that make grandmas so popular with grandchildren.

My mother arrives for an afternoon visit, crisp and bright. Before the children can take the starch out of her, she is crisply and brightly on her way home. She brings bubble gum, cupcakes and breakable toys. She is gone before the time for turpentine, vacuum cleaner and glue. When she comes with my father for Sunday dinner, they both applaud like a Palace Audience as the children demonstrate the week's accomplishments in vocals and acrobatics. But before the feats of talent deteriorate into fits of temper, my parents have smilingly slipped away.

When I was a child, candy and chewing gum were forbidden fruit and bedtime was never postponed. Now the disciplinarian of my youth pleads with me: "Let them stay up just fifteen minutes longer." She never arrives without an armful of gifts and goodies, never leaves without a headful of ideas for future gifts. She is never too busy to read a story or too tired to play first base. And she never says No.

Does Grandma spoil my children? You bet!

That's a grandmother's pleasure and privilege. And even though I may sound as if I don't believe it, it's great for the youngsters, too. I remember with warmth and joy the grandparents who spoiled me. I'm glad my children can bask in the sunny side of an easygoing, easygiving, carefree grandmother. And they reciprocate.

Grandma days are special. Nobody strays far from home when my parents are expected. When my parents' car pulls up, you can hear the shouting for blocks. Even the baby crows fit to burst her romper buttons.

Naturally, I can't expect my children to be so enthusiastic about me. I'm here all the time and I've got work to do. But as I said before, in fifteen years or so, I hope to be a grandmother myself.

"You're having a pretty good time," I remarked to my mother the other day.

"Yes, I am," she agreed. "This is my harvest."

I know just what she meant.

Rollie Hochstein

Grandma Updated

Grandma never takes a look to the front or back,
To suggest that her age may be advancing.
She won't tend the babies for you anymore,
For Grandma is taking up dancing.

She's not content with thinking old thoughts,
With old-fashioned, second-hand knowledge.
Don't bring your mending for Grandma to do,
For Grandma has gone back to college.

Elizabeth Gibson

The Grandmother

When Grandmother comes to our house,
She sits in the chair and sews away.
She cuts some pieces just alike
And makes a quilt all day.

I watch her bite the little thread,
Or stick the needle in and out.
And then she remembers her grandmother's house,
And what her grandmother told about,

And now a very long ago—
She tells it while she cuts and strips—
We used to live in Mary-land,
And there was a water with ships.

But that was long before her day
She says, and so I like to stand
Beside her chair, and then I ask,
"Please tell about in Mary-land."

Elizabeth Madox Roberts

In Maryland

When it was Grandmother Annie's day,
We lived on a hill, and down below,
Beyond the pasture and the trees,
A river used to go.

The water was very wide and blue
And deep, and my! it was a sight
To see the ships go up and down
And all the sails were white

And Grandmother Annie used to wait
Beside the window or the door.
She never was tired of it
To watch the river any more.

And we could hardly see across,
And the water was blue, as blue as the sky,
And all day long and all day long
We watched the little ships go by.

Elizabeth Madox Roberts

Classics From
The Classroom

Oliver Wendell Holmes once observed that "pretty much all the honest truth-telling there is in the world is done by children." I agree. Youngsters have their own opinions and few are hesitant to express them—especially in their essays, which I have collected over the past fifteen years.

Here, fresh from the minds of some nine-year-olds, are some delightfully original observations about grandparents:

"My grandad's name is Joe but he is more important than his name sounds."

"Grandmother is always saying some of the most adsurb truths."

"I know the answer is no when she gives me a long sigh."

"My grandad is six foot 1. He is half Irish half English and half French. He is of an unusually bigly size."

"Sometimes Grandfather tells me to be sure to study so I will be a good scholar. Scholar is a spare word he uses when he cannot think how to say studyer."

"When he starts to tell me a story about one of his friends called Paul Bunyun, I just twinkle an eye. It is a story that is more for saying than believing."

More and more, I'm convinced that the most hilarious comedians in the country are all in grade school. They have a knack of writing with a freshness that no grown-up could possibly match. Here's what I mean:

"For some reason children can have twice as many grandparents as parents. Just because, I guess."

"One of my grandfathers was born in 1912, supposably on his birthday."

"My family consists of my father and my mother and me and Steve and my grandparents down the street. Steve is my brother. Otherwise we are unrelationed."

"I used to save up bugs until mother said don't. Then I collected worms until dad and grandad axidently went fishing with them. Now I am out of collections."

And as for what Holmes called "honest truth-telling" —a bit smudged, to be sure— we subscribe to the following:

"What we should get Grandmother for her birthday is part of everybody's spare thinking these days."

"Grandfather agrees that living expenses today are a redicolous large fact of a number."

And while the Department of Labor is studying that "large fact," let me tell you about a brown-eyed little girl in my class who summed up all her feelings about her grandparents in this way:

"My grandparents can do wonderful things. Like they can put a twig of one tree on to the root of another tree and still have it grow. I will always put both gladness and wonder in my same thought about grandparents."

Me, too.

Harold Dunn

On Being
A Grandmother

*Margaret Mead, the famous an-
thropologist and social historian
exults in a very special child—her
first grandchild. Some of her feelings are universal; some personal.
All are deeply thought provoking.*

On October 9, 1969, I became a grandmother.

Curious! Through no immediate act of my own,
my status was altered irreversibly and for all time.
It is always so, of course. The birth of a child, an
extraordinarily small and fragile creature, changes
one's own place in the world and that of every mem-
ber of a family in ways that cannot be completely
foreseen.

Even when the child's heritage over many generations is known, the child itself is a new person
and unique.

Years ago, long before my own child was born,
I steeled myself against some of the traits I loved
least in my relatives, characteristics a child of mine
might inherit. Like every family, mine had its
anomalies—unexplained great-aunts who had been a
little peculiar, a few individuals with extraordinarily
trivial minds, a whole line of men whose charm was
too great for their own good. My English husband
did not have many living relatives and I had met
only a few of them. Although I had heard scraps of

his family history—stories about one person's oddities and another's distinctions—the things I knew were hardly enough for fear or imagination to feed upon.

I was fortunate in not caring whether the child I was waiting for was a girl or a boy. For if one finds oneself (this is how I feel it is) having a very strong preference for one sex or the other, this makes it much harder to wait for the stranger who will change one's life forever. I thought about the future during those waiting months. In the background was the implicit decision that if the baby was a boy, we would probably live in England, but that if it was a girl, we would live in the United States because a girl would have more freedom in this country. I feel sure that this guided my thoughts just below the surface. But I sternly refused to daydream about the kind of child this baby, yet unborn, might be. I have always been very conscious of how my personal daydreams might affect the life of a child or a student, someone helpless before them.

What has this to do with being a grandmother?

It seems to me that one begins to think about grandchildren from the time one's son or daughter marries. One's daughter-in-law or son-in-law will bring new elements into the line of descent. And then when the first grandchild is expected—especially when the child is a daughter's child, as in my case—one lives again, one step removed, the hopes and fears that accompanied the birth of one's own child, who will now be a parent.

I told myself that I might never see even one grandchild. When my daughter was born I was 38. Some of my classmates were already grandmothers and living to the age of a great-grandmother is not yet something anyone can take for granted. So after my daughter's marriage, while she and her husband were studying and designing a life together, I simply took delight in the present and its promise for the future. I thought of their life as one a child might happily choose to enter.

This sense that a child has somehow chosen its parents is a very deep and old human feeling. It is, I am sure, a feeling we should not lose. It gives a child—one's own child and a child adopted with love—a status as an individual in his own right. And this, I believe, is one of the best gifts we can give children—from the first, the freedom to choose their own path.

Generations

The first matter you will probably need to clarify for the seven-to-twelve-year-olds, whether you are a young grandma or a great-grandmother, is that you were not in the theater when Lincoln was shot and that, while you may have looked well in the long-waisted fashions of the twenties you never wore either hoopskirts or bustles. Even a great-grandmother can just about remember hobble skirts! Today's younger grandmothers heard the cry of "Heigh-ho, Silver," each afternoon over the radio, but it may be necessary to explain that rangers and Indians were not camping on the doorstep even in your distant girlhood. Sorting out the salient points in different eras is more educational for the young than learning to recognize letters of the alphabet at three or reciting number combinations at six.

Few children are bored with tales of the past, especially stories that involve their parents and grandparents, and earlier forebears. Hearing these tales retold aids them in finding their own answers to those puzzling questions, "Who am I?" . . . "What was the world like before I was here?" Going with Grandma to see the house in which Mother or Father lived, if by any chance a house twenty years old has not been demolished, does more than constitute an afternoon's excursion. It helps establish a feeling of continuity between the generations. Solidarity in the family is fostered, too, through looking over old scrapbooks and albums or being allowed to handle or perhaps even possess some relic from a parent or grandparent's childhood. "You are my mommy's mommy? Who was your mommy?" is a fascinating question to the young. If great-grandmother is also on the scene, to understand that she is grandmother's mother, not her sister, is difficult for the youngest children. Old is old to them and they see little distinction between forty-five and seventy.

Edith G. Neisser

Grandma's House

It always smelled so wonderful
Of cookies, cakes and pies;
It always had a secret place
That held a nice surprise!
It had that "homey, lived-in look,"
Was always nice and neat;
It looked a lot like Grandma looked—
So warm, so good, so sweet!
It had a cheery atmosphere,
A certain kind of glow,
That made you happy when you came
And sorry when you'd go!
It always smelled of fresh-picked flowers
She'd gathered from her yard;
It always looked so "spic and span"
Like she had scrubbed it hard!
It was a very special house,
A happy place to go—
Her house was just like Grandma was,
That's why I loved it so!

Helen Farries

Excursions With Grandmother

When I was a boy, she and I took long walks around town in the gold summer dusk, out to the cemetery or miles and miles to the Old Ladies Home, talking in torrents between the long silences. All about us were forests of crape myrtles and old houses faintly ruined. Widow ladies and spinsters sat on the galleries of the dark houses cooling themselves with paper fans, and we greeted each lady by turn, and then she told me who they were and what had happened to their people. We must have been an unlikely pair on those long-ago journeys, she in her flowing dress and straw hat, I barefoot in a T-shirt and blue jeans, with a sailor's cap on my head, separated by our 60 years. Only when I grew older did I comprehend that it was the years between us that made us close; ours was a symbiosis forged by time.

Willie Morris

Summary

If grandmas are great characters, who has a better right—and who enchants the young more? Betty MacDonald, in "The Egg and I," described a grandmother who was dynamically and bravely herself, and the devil take the hindmost.

Gammy was patient, impatient, kind, caustic, witty, sad, wise, foolish, superstitious, religious, prejudiced and dear. She was, in short, a grandmother who is, after all, a woman whose inconsistencies have sharpened with use. I have no patience with women who complain because their mothers or their husbands' mothers have to live with them. To my prejudiced eye, a child's life without a grandparent *en residence* would be a barren thing.

Fanny—
You're Marvelous

Marjorie Kinnan Rawlings gave us a portrait of a woman who carried her love and nonsense triumphantly into grandmotherhood, when she wrote "Fanny— You Fool!"

All my life I have watched beautiful women in the manner of a small boy peering in a pastry window. Women were surely intended to be beautiful, and it is a low trick on the part of Creation to make some of them ravishing and to give Phi Beta Kappa keys to the rest of us as a sop. It is only as middle age has moved in that I have discovered the compensations of being born "plain." The greatest of these is that where the glamour girls of my generation have lost all, I and my kind have had nothing to lose. And a great understanding has dawned on me, as well, that the beautiful woman has a certain philosophy that makes her desirable. This philosophy may be had by any woman. My maternal grandmother possessed the quality in the highest degree.

Fanny was not beautiful. She was too small and too impudent. She was pretty, and I think the prettiness itself came largely from the impudence. She was five feet two at most, pleasantly plump, with naturally curly hair and eyes as blue as an April sky and with the peculiar wickedness of a kitten's. But what gave her her charm was what Grandfather called her foolishness.

Many a woman would have lost all charm under the circumstances of her life. She came of Michigan pioneer stock, as did Grandfather. They were married when she was sixteen and he was nineteen. He had his own inherited farm of some two hundred acres, and they set out, a pair of children, by our notions, to make a life. Grandfather, to the day of his death at eighty-odd, was always fatuously enamoured of her. Abe was six feet four, lean and awkward, with no sense of humour with which to defend himself against her superabundance of it.

She played one practical joke with never-failing success on her sober husband. He would drive to the village on business, and returning at dusk, drooped in all his length and brooding earnestness over the reins, would see a white-sheeted apparition jump out from the bushes under the heads of the horses. The horses never became accustomed to Fanny's nonsense, either, and would bolt and run with satisfying regularity. Arriving at the house, the horses at last under control and stabled, Abe would find Fanny rocking placidly and would storm in on her, shouting, "Fanny—you fool!"

Typically, Fanny delighted in telling it on him that, for all his Puritan severity, he loved to have her play the hussy. On these occasions, again, he would rise, even in old age, from his chair and bellow, "Fanny—you fool!" Then he would subside and sit watching her by the hour, unaware that his grave face was luminous with his idolatry.

He was not alone in his adoration. Her kitchen, her pantry, her cellar, her dining-table, enslaved her grandchildren. She managed her household and her cuisine with casual efficiency. I have never, at any great table, amateur or professional, eaten more delicious food than she served daily as a matter of course.

The food would account for the devotion of Fanny's grandchildren. But, above all, we loved her for her absurd tricks. Of many of them I dare not tell. But I remember that in her latter years we made excuses to invite strange children into the house, solely to show off one of her accomplishments. She would be sitting innocently and would suddenly and unconcernedly protrude her false teeth and roll her eyes at the visitors. This appalling picture invariably brought shrieks of delight. From Abe it brought, out of habit, the old "Fanny—you fool!" Then he would beam at her.

The key to Fanny is that she was sublimely herself. She was not indifferent to those who worshipped her, certainly, or she would not have played so to the gallery. But she quite simply went her own way, saucy, ribald—and took admiration for granted. It came to her as a moth flies to the flame. The point of view is natural to a beautiful woman. I recommend it as well to the merely pretty and to the plain.

First Time

The new house has a most astonished air.
With curtains wrinkled and with blinds awry,
No longer trimly neat, it seems to stare
With curiously apprehensive eye
At little girls who leave mud pies to scorch
Upon its steps while chasing little boys
All up and down the uprights of its porch
With clamorous, before unheard-of-noise.
There's ample reason for its glassy gaze;
It's new and unprepared for manic stunts
And its owner never before in all its days
Had six grandchildren visiting at once!

Jane Merchant

Visiting
The Grandparents

We know that few grandparents are severe. Parents have to take this into account. Ponder the interview with a young mother who has survived several visits home with her children. She makes it a practice never to let the kids know too far ahead of time that they're going to visit Grandma and Grandpa, because they get all stirred up and out of hand. Once they're actually at their grandparents' house, however, they get out of hand anyway.

"Then who disciplines them?" asked the reporter.

"Jim and I do," answered the mother, "but it isn't easy on account of the sneaking."

"Did you say streaking?" asked the reporter.

"No, sneaking. You know, like when I send the kids to their room and then either my mother or father sneaks up and consoles them with cookies or something."

"Doesn't that spoil them?"

"Not really," said the mother. "Once we get home, we can usually get things back to normal in a week or so if we work on it."

Anonymous

Grandma Is A Swinger

It is increasingly difficult to distinguish the grandmothers from the mothers these days. Grandparents
have a new look. I asked a group of nursery children: "What do grandmothers and grandfathers
do?" "Go shopping," they told me. "And play golf
and tennis and go swimming. They dance and go to
the office and go to meetings. Sometimes they tell
stories. They go bowling. They make lots of
money." That's what grandparents do.

Eda J. LeShan

Grandma's Day

My grandma takes her shower
    At the very crack of dawn,
And she never fails to fix her hair
    Or put her makeup on.
Then she drives down on the freeway
    In a bright blue Thunderbird,
To a building called a courthouse,
    Where she has the final word.
When the bailiff sees her coming,
    He gives the clerk a nudge,
'Cause you see, my grandma truly is
    A most superior judge.

But when the sun is going down
    And court's at last adjourned,
My grandma has a slew of things
    With which she's most concerned.
Sometimes she bakes an apple pie.
    Sometimes she frosts a cake.
When she does that, I lick the bowl—
    That is, if I'm awake.
But the nicest part of Grandma's day,
    Is when the lights are dim,
And she comes tip-toe up the stairs
    To see that I'm tucked in.

Lee Sobelman

Descriptions

Dorothy Barclay, gathering material for the article, "How to Succeed as Grandma," came up with some descriptions not of what a grandmother should be, but of what some are.

"A good grandmother is calm and quiet," an 8-year-old boy said. "You never see her do the shopping, but there's always good stuff to eat. She's not busy all the time. And even when she is busy, she's not *so* busy. You can come in the kitchen when she's cooking and she'll talk to you."

"You can have fun at a grandmother's house," a 6-year-old boy reported. "She isn't always telling you 'watch out.' She has ideas about things to do and she takes you places. Also she lets you spend your dollar for what you want. But if you spent it all for candy she wouldn't let you eat it all at once."

"I have three grandmothers," said a worldly 7-year old. "The one I like best has lots of things that are different, not like what we have at home. She gives me my milk from a pitcher that's like a rooster and all her dishes have different flowers painted on them. She has a lot of things I have to be careful when I touch. They are very pretty."

Other marvelous definitions were given to Lee Parr McGrath and Joan Scobey for their book, "What Is a Grandmother?"

My grandmother is a groovy person. She rides a honda. She is married to a grandfather.

Timmy

I sometimes have to protect my grandmother when my mother scolds her.

Grace

A grandma is made to spoil you and save you from your parents.

Andy

Grandmothers play with you whether they are busy or not. That's why a grandmother is my kind of person.

Margaret

Since Grandma
Took Up Golf

Since Grandma took up golf, she gets
    Out early in the day;
And with her oldest grandchild, Ruth,
    She sallies forth to play.
There's lot of talk of bunkers now,
    And much on teeing off;
And all the kids are interested
    Since Grandma took up golf.

Since Grandma took up golf, she wears
    A sweater bright but neat;
And when she talks of greens, you bet,
    It's not the kind you eat!
We thought perhaps the neighborhood
    Behind its blinds might cough;
But they all think it's just the thing
    That Grandma took up golf.

Since Grandma took up golf, somehow
    We young folks have more pep.
That this is quite a jolly world
    We're just now getting hep.
We can not count our age by years;
    The spirit—don't you scoff!
Old age has lost its fears for me
    Since Grandma took up golf!

Anne Campbell

Super-Gram

Grandmothers do more than romp and play. The thing that can be almost frightening to a younger woman is that they do it so well. Jean Kerr describes her mother's energy in "Please Don't Eat the Daisies."

My mother came to help us move. This was a great boon, except that there is something wrong with her metabolism. She is not able to work for more than nineteen hours without stopping. During this period she is sustained by nothing more than several gallons of hot tea, which she consumes while on the top rungs of ladders or deep inside crates. By midnight, when I was ready to sob with fatigue, it was nothing for Mother to announce cheerfully, "Well, what do you say we clean out the garage?" She was a little disconcerted, though, when she discovered she wasn't able to pick up a television set, and I heard her moaning softly, "Jean, I'm afraid I'm beginning to slow down." I don't know whether it's true, but we can hope.

The Joyful Time

Youth fades: love droops; the lesson of friendship falls;
A mother's secret hope outlives them all.

Oliver Wendell Holmes

What the mother was probably hoping, all the time she was enduring parenthood, was that her children would some day marry and produce children of their own. For then begins a magical time for a woman—the time of being most completely herself—of being a grandmother . . . .

I remember Mary Alice. She belonged to the generation of women who raised their children hygienically and sent them out into the world, then tinted their hair blue and spent their afternoons playing cards.

Mary Alice didn't fancy blue hair and cards bored her. So she followed her children out into the world. She went back to work, and we were all under the impression that motherhood had been only an interruption in a brisk business career. But then her first grandchild was born. She neglected her work to make receiving blankets when the child was expected. She resurrected from the attic her own christening dress when the baby was baptized.

And one day I found her standing and holding the baby, swaying back and forth as if she were a sea captain whose ship was riding out some gentle swells. The effect on the baby was beatific. He had his head pillowed on Mary Alice's not-too-ample bosom. He was crooning as if he had just consumed a whole nursing bottle full of soothing syrup.

"I had three kids before I learned to rock like this," said Mary Alice, "but it's like riding a bicycle. Once you've gotten the knack, you never forget how."

Mary Carey

Bedtime Talks

At night, before sleep comes, I sometimes have imaginary talks with my grandchildren. I tell them:

One day we'll see the old country together: the cathedrals of Köln and Strassburg, of Chartres and York. We will stroll along the wall of an English garden in springtime; along a Dutch gracht with the stiff patrician houses mirrored in the quiet water; along a German village street at dusk when wood smoke curls up over red roofs, cows come home tinkling their bells, and children sing and play among the old gravestones in the churchyard. I will take you to the house in which Goethe was born in my hometown, Frankfurt. In '45 this house was a heap of rubble: Reverence for a great poet has raised it from the ashes. It is one of the sacred places of mankind, like Shakespeare's house in Stratford-on-Avon, like the Parthenon, like the honey-colored temples of Paestum. You will know why, because you have read books, have looked at pictures; and we have talked about what you have read and seen.

You will know about your own country also, because your mother will have read you Thomas Wolfe's and other writers' hymns to America, this country that is young and new compared with the land your grandparents came from. America, the country in which out of the seething mixture of people from all continents, all races, all creeds—God willing—one day the Free Man will be born; and you will have to do your part to make this dream come true.

Don't live so quickly. Take time for things that matter. Don't believe in the new idea called high-living standard. True values will not be found in things money can buy. They are in love, friendship, duty, truth. You may find them between the two covers of a book, in a Mozart andante, a view from a mountain peak, a stanza of a poem, the smile of a strange child. These are the things that will count when one day you draw the sum of your life.

Thus I talk to my grandchildren at night, before sleep comes: to serious-minded David; to Norman, bubbling with vitality; and to first-grader Alan. Perhaps, I think, there is something after all which I may pass on. Perhaps, I hope, it shall not have been in vain that I was a grandmother.

Margot Benary-Isbert

The
Absence

My grandmother left this morning.
    She's going to travel in Spain.
I asked my mother and my dad
    When she'll be home again.

And who will bake my gingersnaps
    And take me on my walks?
Who will read and sing to me?
    Who'll listen when I talk?

Both my mother and my dad
    Are very nice, you see,
But sometimes they forget the way
    It is when you are three.

My grandma knows the secrets.
    They twinkle in her eyes.
She's just as smart as little kids,
    And that is really wise!

Lee Sobelman

Relax . . . Enjoy!

Lavinia Russ describes the special relationship between grandmother and grandchild—and the joy of being a grandmother—in her book, "A High Old Time."

. . . to be any kind of grandmother is to be a very happy woman. It's the most relaxed role of all the many parts a woman plays in her life. She doesn't have the responsibility of the grandchild, so that he or she comes under the heading of pure velvet. She is not responsible for the child's manners, except to serve as an exemplary illustration to follow. She would interrupt a bishop's sermon before a child's story. She has the leisure to listen. She has the time to take a grandson to lunch, to ask him to order and play the host. She has it in her power to make every visit a party, if she is a wise grandmother, who is aware of how much the young and old have in common. They share a sense of wonder. To a child his first ride on a ferryboat is a new and astonishing experience. To a grandmother who hasn't taken the time from a crowded life to go aboard, it's a delightful event. Neither is concerned with power or position, money or the future. To children, tomorrow is a million years away. Today is the only reality. Instinct has given them that wisdom. Long years of living have revealed it to their grandmothers.

Freed of the necessity to instruct or guide, a grandmother can laugh with her grandchildren at all the absurdities they both see and hear together. (She will never laugh at her grandchildren's mistakes; ridicule for the young can be as lethal as carbon monoxide.) Together they can scorn the false and the phony. Children have a finely-tuned antenna for the phony; the old have learned by experience to detect it.

They both believe in the invisible. The young accept the existence of mythical creatures that they can't see; the old, a God, or the good in man that they can't behold. The young have forgotten yesterday. The old remember it as history and like to return to it in stories of the old days. Small children relish these stories so long as they are histories, not moral tracts. To them, you are a visitor from another planet. You can answer their question, "What was it like there?"

Set in Caledonia, roman and italic.
Designed by Publishers Graphics.
Illustrated by Harold R. Frenck.

Acknowledgments

The editor and the publisher have made every effort to trace the ownership of all copyrighted material and to secure permission from copyright holders of such material. In the event of any question arising as to the use of any material the publisher and editor, while expressing regret for inadvertent error, will be pleased to make the necessary corrections in future printings. Thanks are due to the following authors, publishers, publications and agents for permission to use the material indicated.

ABINGDON PRESS, for "Takeover" from *Because It's Here* by Jane Merchant, copyright © 1970 by Abingdon Press.

BELL-McCLURE SYNDICATE, for "Since Grandma Took Up Golf" by Anne Campbell.

MARGOT BENARY-ISBERT, for "At Night Before Sleep Comes," copyright © 1968 by Margot Benary-Isbert.

BRANDT & BRANDT, for "Fanny—You Fool!" by Marjorie Kinnan Rawlings, copyright 1942 by Marjorie Kinnan Rawlings, renewed © 1970 by Norton Baskin.

CHANGING TIMES, The Kiplinger Magazine, for excerpt from November 1974 issue, copyright 1974 by The Kiplinger Washington Editors, Inc.

CURTIS BROWN, LTD., for "Grandmothers Get All the Breaks" by Rollie Hochstein, reprinted from the March 1964 issue of *Good Housekeeping* © 1964 by The Hearst Corporation; for excerpt from *Ox Bells and Butterflies*, by Ernest Buckler, copyright © 1968 by Ernest Buckler.

DOUBLEDAY & COMPANY, INC., for excerpt from "The Kerr Hilton," copyright 1955 by The Curtis Publishing Company, from *Please Don't Eat the Daisies* by Jean Kerr.

HAROLD DUNN, for "Classics from the Classroom."